human/nature poems

tracie morris

human / nature poems

litmus press
2023

ISBN: 978-1-93395-964-1

LCCN: 2023005543

Cataloging-in-Publication data is available from the Library of Congress.

Design and typesetting by Kit Schluter
Cover art by Jemman: "The Greys," 2023 and "Within Clouds," 2023

Litmus Press is a program of Ether Sea Projects, Inc., a 501(c)(3) non-profit literature and arts organization.

Litmus Press publications are made possible by the New York State Council on the Arts with support from Governor Kathy Hochul and the New York State Legislature. This project is also supported in part by an award from the National Endowment for the Arts and by public funds from the New York City Department of Cultural Affairs in partnership with the City Council. Additional support for Litmus Press comes from the Leslie Scalapino–O Books Fund, The Post-Apollo Press, individual members and donors. All contributions are fully tax-deductible.

LITMUS PRESS
925 Bergen Street #405
Brooklyn, New York 11238
litmuspress.org

SMALL PRESS DISTRIBUTION
1341 Seventh Street
Berkeley, California 94710
spdbooks.org

contents

introduction

IN *HUMAN/NATURE POEMS*, TRACIE MORRIS RECORDS THE ALLUSIVE meditations and associative leaps of an agile mind moving through the world with embodied awareness. The scope of this poetry collection is wide-ranging: domestic settings in the U.S. with human interlocutors matching wits, or people speaking to, for, and about inanimate objects and non-human beings (birds, trees, snowflakes, afro-bushy houseplants, misplaced tube socks, vibrating stones); travel notes collected on trips to Africa, Asia, Europe, and Latin America; personal reflections on collective and individual memory and identity; eclectic poems inspired by Allen Ginsberg and John Ashbery, Toni Morrison and Ishmael Reed, Ezra Pound and Ralph Ellison, Raymond Patterson and Duriel Harris, Jo Stewart, Kurt Schwitters and Dick Higgins, Stevie Wonder and The 5th Dimension (featured in *Summer of Soul*), Brittney Griner, Harriet Tubman (Araminta Ross), and Emmett Till, "Mamie's murdered son"; collaborative writing with partners from Charles Bernstein to Wikipedia pages; and poems shaped by the influence of Japanese traditions of prose and poetry writing. *human/nature poems* is all that, and more, dressed up and dressed down in bespoke vernaculars, fluent allusions, and the poetic cryptic-crossword diction of the inimitable Tracie Morris. A pleasure for the reader is digging deeper into a density of signification accumulated and compressed, like geologic layers, in this poet's work.

Attentive to the human being's subjectivity interacting with the physical world's materiality, this poet's perspectives are local and global. The work unites hemispheres of earth and brain as it incorporates a wondering mind in a wandering body. How do we impose our will on the physical world? How do we acclimate to variable conditions? Regarding the movement of human consciousness in space and time, an implicit focus of the poet's attention is the always-shifting interplay of subjects and objects as groups and individuals respond to changing environments: gentrifying neighborhoods, travel destinations, seasonal variations, the anthropogenically altered earth.

This interrelation of inside and outside figures early in the collection, with "Inside Winter." The title refers to a housebound speaker, observing winter's snowfall, as well as the poem's drilling into a frozen core of memory marked by economic insecurity and collective ingenuity. The speaker takes a certain emotional risk, recalling childhood from an adult perspective: "I stick my head out." A snowy landscape, with the colors of surviving but "muted" birds, parallels the simulated winter inside a refrigerator-freezer, "standard issue project box," chilling budget-friendly "chicken we cut from whole."

Crystalline structures of individual falling snowflakes contrast with "snow fluff" formed in a bargain-basement fridge without a frost-free guarantee. The poem juxtaposes fond recollection, the wonder of winter experienced by children catching snowflakes on their tongues, with the practical daily reality of struggling and striving adults whose environmental concerns prioritize immediate survival.

The speaker of *human/nature* is seasonally affected by "the sky's mood," registering fluctuations in temperature and barometric pressure, alert to changing climate. An environmentally and culturally conscious migrant, descended (like many Black Americans) from uprooted Africans and dislocated Native Americans, the speaker in "Down to Feathers, Skin, Bone: American Acclimatization Metaphor" notes the unintended consequences of migrating humans introducing themselves and other exotic species into new habitats while ignoring ecological impact in favor of cultural preferences. Like Shakespeare's works, invasive English sparrows that displace native birds are successful exports, if measured by their ability to compete in their adopted settings.

In several poems, the speaker associates chilly winters and slow-thawing springs with overcast skies and clouds of grey (British spelling), as in the poem "It's taking a while for the grey light…," along with "the grey outside, / spring grey" in "Acclimate," and the "Grey mottling sea" of the Atlantic Middle Passage in "Prism":

> How did we get here?
> How do we go, Black?

Grey in relation to Black might seem watered down: "close enough to Black fading?" England's grey light stands in contrast to the "ever / lasting" light of Egypt's Cairo and Luxor where "Sol has hands," a reference to ancient Egyptian representation of the sun's benevolent rays as radiating arms with hands outstretched. (Such comparisons may break down as climate change creates extreme conditions worldwide. Flights were redirected from UK airport runways that melted in the heat of summer 2022.)

As a visitor to "Anglaterra," with its natural and human-built wonders, from The Needles, a chalky landform in the English Channel at Isle of Wight, to the ancient circle of Stonehenge, the poetic speaker contemplates an extended timeline of the nascent nation before its history as an acquisitive empire. On the Isle of Wight, the speaker communes with the spirit of Arwald, known as the last pagan king of Anglo-Saxon England. Killed in battle, his sons executed as prisoners of war, his sister's offspring sired by a rival king, her name lost to history, Arwald and his kin represent Britain's pagan past. The poetic speaker empathizes with the pagan's plight, lamenting Arwald's demise, his sister's captive womb: "Yes, I shudder at this too, Arwald. Centuries of my myriad mothers know her / wails." Morris traces this conquered pagan spirit, in poetic travel notes, back through the history and prehistory of the United Kingdom.

Traveling in England, the poetic speaker is a visitor to Stonehenge, a mysterious prehistoric monument, a circular arrangement of roughly rectangular megaliths, preserved as a national heritage site and tourist destination on the Salisbury Plain of Wiltshire. In addition to its construction in alignment with annual solar and lunar events, the acoustical properties of Stonehenge may be of interest to Morris, known for her innovative sound poetry that exceeds "experiment" in its engagement with issues of social justice. Apparently straying off the visitors' path to breach the protected perimeter of Stonehenge, the speaker combines the insouciance of a subway-fare-jumping scofflaw with a worldly tourist's skepticism—"I didn't notice much / magic about the land. I wondered above it"—and the ritual acts of a pilgrim visiting a sacred place, absorbing the reverberations of its vibrating stones.

The text of *human/nature poems* is further influenced by Japanese traditions of prose and poetry writing: zuihitsu, encompassing loosely connected personal reflections, improvisational prose, journal entries, and evocative lists (notably in *The Pillow Book [Makura no Sōshi]* of Sei Shōnagon); haibun, alternating passages of prose with haiku to trace a journey (exemplified in *The Narrow Road to the Interior*, or *The Narrow Road to the Deep North [Oku no Hosomichi]*, by Matsuo Bashō). Modern haibun may include diaristic literary prose writing, such as travel notes, vignettes, and autobiographical sketches, alternated with obliquely-related minimalist poetry verses, tanka, haiku, or senryu. With contemporary variations on haibun and zuihitsu, through domestic meditations and notes of an observant world traveler, Morris demonstrates the practice of writing as a road connecting exterior and interior.

HARRYETTE MULLEN
Los Angeles, 2022

preface: reflective glass

I BEGAN GATHERING THIS COLLECTION DURING MY THREE-MONTH quarantine after being hospitalized with COVID in the Spring of 2020. That frightening and enlightening spring and summer helped me to see a few things more clearly—some recent things, others I hadn't thought about in decades.

Firstly, being on strict quarantine gave me a different sense of space and time, as the pandemic did for everyone, globally. Secondly, I experienced the urban natural environment, the non-human environment differently: through glass. Because the COVID diagnosis was, at that time, very mysterious and often very deadly, I kept my windows largely shut except for cracks. The windows at once became an opening for communion and a barrier, as all windows can be, and yet writ large without direct human interaction. They also became magnifiers of what was outside and what was within. (As I write this in the winter of 2023, the air is grey again and warmer than usual and coincidentally reflects my state of mind as I began what would become this book. Apt setting for a preface.)

Funny—strange—enough, I also discovered my "muscle memory" while I was COVID-confined: as an infant and into childhood I was severely ill with several maladies that left me intermittently bedridden. This disruptive and indelible time of my formative years forced an early reconciliation with time, space, breath and connection. Turns out it was a fruitful experience in the long run. I became an even more avid reader (I was an early and precocious self-starter), thinker and dreamer. Decades later I "remembered" that I had this somatic and conceptual knowledge/experience regarding isolation and, somehow, well actually *because* of poetry, the glass held and the walls began to dissolve everywhere, even as I longed to feel the wind across my whole self, in its element, outdoors.

What is barometric pressure literally and poetically? When the extraordinary Harryette Mullen generously consented to write the introduction to this book, she noticed my choice of spelling "grey" words with "e"s instead of "a"s (i.e., gray). I said that concretely (as in, concrete poetry) the "e" looks like an "eye" and the heavy lid of the eye is the pressure experienced during COVID phase one. The pressure on us apart and secluded, untouched and holding onto ourselves for comfort. There are all kinds of heavy, we noticed, during this twilighted winter of one full year. As testing became more accurate and vaccines began to get distributed in the fall of 2020, and with the second COVID winter passed through, things opened up somewhat, in some places, with ensuing circumspection. Simultaneously, the frustration at the continued murder and display of Black people by law enforcement and vigilantes resulted in protests throughout the clarifying 2020 summer. My vulnerability precluded my engagement in that healthful community catharsis and power, yet I felt the vibrations through the window. The fact that those protests did not result in significant COVID outbreaks demonstrated the lovingkindness of the activists and advocates for each other and the world (people almost uniformly wore protective masks and practiced other protocols including distributing free sanitizers, gloves, etc., to the marchers) was embedded in their righteousness for one of the "least of these," George Floyd.

The plan is always to get through it to get past it. We're not past anything yet, but we will not be less than our great selves, and we do not give up. We take care: of each other, of ourselves. We speak truth to power. Always have. *(If I have to tell you who "we" is, ask yourself if it's really you?)*

"I'm heated!" I love African-Americanisms. Always specific. Transferring that internal fire to action, and that shouted inferno to words on paper: art and legislation, including anti-us legislation because our power in advocacy has so shaken up those who hate freedom, truth, sharing and generosity. *Dey lost.* They will lose.

Another one of my/our faves: "I feel ya." Reviewing this manuscript and its evocation of my somatic agility/fragility resuscitated memories from deep wells. The poem, "Snapshot: Baby Bikini Et Al," recalled a dated family photo taken when I couldn't have been more than four years old. At the beach, I remember. I recall how much my brother played in the water as I was too full to do anything but lie down, how the barely technicolor photo and memory invoked a cousin who drowned before I was born. He had vitiligo and was a friend, as well as relative, of my mother's. Crashing waves later, my grown brother "crashing" with me right after Sandy hit, the crush of memories swirling with just us in the house. Somehow it's all exalted, somehow it's all very tangible and *right here*. The blowout of nuclear winter and destruction of the Atoll with bomb testing: the butterfly wings of anthropocene arrogance. Mother Nature's climatic blowback. The heat *and* the humidity.

This collection of poems also reflects my heightened connection to what Blackness is, in my view, and what it means to be a global citizen. I am and have always felt both and don't see them as contradictory because I wasn't raised to think of Blackness provincially. However, the tangible nature of being a global citizen (as well as reiterating how the United States is inherently global) is not simply a belief, it is rooted in place, the actual air outside of this country, the invisible *there*, the people, the everything of it, *the moment* one is there and all the moments before then. Having been a world traveler for decades now, sometimes scrimping to barely cover room, board and travel, other times being paid by someone else to visit, I felt my emotional tendrils reaching out to the people I've met, the energy of these places and their continued resonances within and outside. They are always with me and their presence has sometimes brought me back to my self, brought me to tears.

I guess a coda would be okay here: Not so much an elephant in the room but more like a bunny rabbit munching on a carrot in the corner of the house, I've been, and consider myself, a page-based poet always and first. Some people are kind enough to think of me at all, and often when they do, it's for sonic poetry and other types of improvised performance. This book is significant to me not because it's my first book of poetry, but because it's my first book of poetry published in the United States that wasn't en route to the page-based poetry book I wanted to write: it's the book itself. Each of my books stand on their own, I hope, and yet, I'm not sure whether it's because of age, confidence, acceptance or what, I'm letting go of some of my anxiety regarding page poetry collections and simply letting it exist without apology, knowing, as always, that I want to, need to, improve my writing, my relationship with writing, for the rest of my life.

Here are a couple shout outs: Thanks to the delightful posse at Litmus, esp. E. Tracy Grinnell, Rachael Wilson with Alysia Slocum riding shotgun. Big thanks to Kit Schluter for the eagle-eyed errata-catching and lovely design. Thanks to Jemman for the gorgeous, gorgeous cover art. I don't know how you magically encapsulated the book! I loathe to say a picture is worth a thousand words, since, you know, I like words the most, but those two pieces do succinctly sum up the whole book! Thanks to all the folks who published these poems in various journals and such (see my acknowledgements) and all my dear friends and family who support me. I also want to thank my students and colleagues who through their excellence and sincerity have encouraged me, not just in my writing but in hope for poetry and poetics going forward. And if we have hope in poetry, we have hope in the whole world. The world is poetry, all in the world is poetic.

TRACIE MORRIS
Brooklyn, 2023

In my failure is all hope of discovery
and transcendence.

The perfect word has no footing. It
can't be insured against hidden defect.

It's more dangerous than its
circumstances.

It's a demigod. It might not risk its life
for me. Would I risk mine for it?

DJELLOUL MARBROOK,
from "Ball Bearing of the Logos"

setting the scenario

Inside Winter

It's a grey sky today. The expectant birds' colors muted.

We all feel the barometric difference
between snow and rain clouds in winter. I stick my head out.

When I was young it'd be to flick snow
past the body of my tongue, see

if I could feel it melt beyond the blade. Now I'm less
inclined to be amused by each flake's pattern. I can

make my own snow inside my fridge. Worn at the edges
from my constant pulling. Pushing the door before

the vegetables soften, the iceberg, the wintergreen crunch
of stalks. After days organicity betrays the lack of pest

-icides. Above them thickening cubes, in trays. My cheap
freezer. Crystals form around the raked division between motor

and insulate. I used to scrape my hand up there when I could
reach it as a kid. A snow fluff. Magic made in the standard issue

project variety box. Around the too-long-there peas, an enclosed hunk
of meat, it's gristle. Between checks we'd thaw that. It was another

color than bought. The dye infused in the lower-rung brand at
the just past bodega sized market. Genera of something to taste up

lima beans, a congealing soup, pulled apart on top of rice with something as the side. A chicken we cut from whole, up front. Sharp knife in the drawer saving us

half the price of pre-divided parts in sectioned cling styrofoams.

There are degrees of wealth, of poverty, class depending. Separated vs. together. Different tastes of snow. The birds one hand feeds, a luxury.

The kind that feed you. My head and froze cuticles came out smell something that reminds me of what used to like ice, what's still, stews.

It's taking a while for the grey light

1.

to segue. The eve's amber tucked
in a hound dog's jowl. Something's
off about the sky's mood. Like G-d
like Osiris is still considering if we're
thrown to Seth or Ra

Sol has hands in Cairo, in Luxor
today He Rises. I wonder where
the outstretch lands. It matters, knot
what circles your head. What your
kin says is power. Aspects of ever
lasting light, life is all ways made from parting.

My first trek to Anglaterra
I notice how stark the whiffs of white
separate strong beams. They
gather further north, rays insist
through. I realize DeMille's shaft cyclopses,

what these sharp sun slices might mean, made it heaven.
Mists break and gathering toward the Pole. Driving
around Redding, then Stonehenge lay lines,
I didn't notice much
magic about the land, I wondered above it.

2.

When we poets arrive then at the stone circle
a half-hearted rope garlanded 'round.
From North-ish, my custom is to peer
steel-eyes jump turnstiles, far back as
thick metal and neon sun types.
Usain had nothing on determined youth

to rush-hour trains. More modest, hopping links, I sat
on a Wiltshire vibrating slab. Turning toward, pupils in
that edge, out of depth. Not my weft,
yet something any human knows.
Later, at Wight's Needles I'd sense more nestling.

3.

Kyoto tremors come from voices. Fuji-
san signals me one winter. BK behavior has me
climb another loop-chain locals take to heart, respect.
I had no restraint: being so so foreign, Black, *called by vast him*, intimate.
Winter wisps, the air's loosening, I lay on mount's deserted road, humming.

4.

No one ever knows why they wind ways to Sedona.
Why Notre Dame, even afterfire, tuning forks your inner ear.
Why Nara's deer escort you, Melbourne's burrowed wombat pulls you there.
Uganda sails you to the brimming womb, Cairo's mother.
Pious formations at Machu Piccu, Cusco pockets your atmospheric reverie.
Teotihuacan's Temples of Sun and Moon are in your line of eye.

Grey, caulis, cruciform clouds
Peat-color bark, roseate flowers sandstone you can't get a pin in
Callidity in the Valley of Kings, Nubia Queens
Still air, verdigris, oval-cast leaves front slate, sunset.

Nighttime is the _____ time

I saw things in my house. Things I'd bought:
A series of plants that make a sculptured imprint in air, my still
African art, a cheap trinket I bought for this year's Eastern Lunar.

The Rat is supposed to be new. It is. Sometimes I see my cat's
eyes scurry to a corner and I wonder what's there. The precision
of the look. Once I got on the ground behind one so close the
twitched ears began to lie, I wondered what spectrum of sight he
had that saw what thing move. He don't blink but as the whiskers
fritter with his breath there's a silence of knowing that trains him
to eat or play with something to death.

I notice unattributable breezes at home. Windows closed, ivy
shivers along the top, even the heavy-edged snake one that
defies gravity, bamboo one, asparagus struggling to fern.
The sticks in them a reminder of dry days, almost straw among
the small pinprick leaves. A poinsettia with holiday paper still around it.
A festive time. Besides those small wind tunnels everything is immobile.
Except for whiskers everything stilted. Except for what I can't see,
nothing pulses.

Acclimate

Windows solace the grey outside,
spring grey. I've been hearing songs
of avians unfamiliar. It hasn't rained
tamping dust, so haze diffuses ivory
brick home extensions.

A panoramic view here of backs of things:
homes, nests, geese veering. Inside here white
squares sharpen the bark my silled African statues are
made from. They look like me, my kind. My body.

Some diademed. Some nude. Some have the shape
people pay lots for. My plants, to tell the truth, didn't all start
as seedlings. One came gorgeous bushy. Crown of deep
purpler, striped green leaves known for wandering. I confess
I got it due to its looks: a chlorophomatic 'fro. Gives me pleasure.

Through glass, a small family has made a yard out
of their extended roof. A tot goes to play, doggies bark and in the late afternoon
the father goes out there by himself to clean the iota of poop using
an eco-friendly disposable green bag over, over. He's always alone

picking up that detritus. Reverse grim reaper as he bends down
taking up what's used. Grateful to be separate from him, his
choices and the smiles I see from here as the child embraces
bars along parameters of the drop.

Down to Feathers, Skin, Bone: American Acclimatization Metaphor*
(via wi   dia)

1.

star s   mark this   common North America follow. A Society's introduction of
  the century   group in New York City trod European fauna   both

cultural reasons. "   foreign varieties may be useful or interesting"   impact history
of North   , due to invasive s s.   Paris   Saint- Acclimatation

et domestication des animaux ("Acclimatization Domestication Useful   ") urge French
  to introduce, breed, provide meat to control . The inspired

groups around , in countries colonized by Europe   before American society's founding,
    wealthy   residents   introduce foreign s   Central Park   had   black s.

European s "multiplied amazingly" others not   as well. efforts redouble
annual meeting report   s   the release of 50 pairs of English   only a success,

across   to   New   Brooklyn.   Europ a, Japanese p easants,   were noted.
  adjourned group resolve to introduce European tits—"   useful to the farmer

contribute to beauty of the fields." acist as chair. Another member, silk ,   boxes
  Manhattan to breed.

2.

an avid admirer of Shakespeare,   the society's force   resolve an aesthetic goal
    introduce the Bard's works.   society's wildest success   the European talent

      king. *"give it him, to keep his anger still in motion."*

The American poet wrote his poem ("winged settler has his place/With race") at best,
a lunatic .   society's effort described "infamous"   "most notorious introduction"

cultural: "Western European settlers from their homelands in new environs." some released
    before society was founded, 100 more   . By   early 21st century,

200 million European s   spread the United States, Mexico and Canada   aggressive
    collapse of native   s, state, the eastern . the decline of local s

European   world's worst invasive species.   the European called society "the canonic
    cautionary tale of biological pollution"

      the most reviled   blamed for helping spread plan s   , ivy disrupting air

---

* spaces not to scale

401 Requiem

1.

There's a sign near the waterfront
I think it's advertising cheer:
saying 400 years, VIRGINIA SPIRITS. A swig.

A year ago last night, my dead crowd me
an evening ceremony
of Jamestown, at the schooner

that brought those first here.
They think: long trip
did not yet know, not the longest part

hairpin turns 'head:
The exact day's alignment,
if the moon bled that defining night. Wisp

of clouds. Was sunset
golden? I'm sitting
yards away. Feel pulling

Brooklyn cemetery, south east. I'd been
with friends, white from out
of town just before. We marvel

at the dock's sky hues, pinking, baby's breath, the water's
iris of the narrow, soft cotton scenes
atmosphere, the svelte lede.

Back, many birds fight for food
at the edge of my home
underfloor people

drywall crates upon another
comfortably laying
in canopy until the next storm

hits, a sandy conflagration of shore and concrete,
or other setback of colluding elements. The birds are
notes along the rail. They see inside.

2.

Temporal extension of a pine
greets me sees
expectant: "I'm waiting for you—

to do something." Who waits on the side
as larger birds, gulls: feast, fight, spring
from earth, flailed wings.

Below, sparrow and finch grow fat
off my spread, little grains left
by ague grey doves. Deserved largess.

Various avians fix pennons,
peck to make others, move
sparrows, occlude, recede to floor

eat under hangings
chirping toward each other in shadow
of bigger feathered arms.

I give the little things to gobble, don't waver. Even
with them "I over cook," make too much.
The worst thing a Black woman can do:

not have enough food for whomever she might feed.
I fit so this peaceful instant its verily
wishing through a lover of sun—as

though a latch on the other side sprung.

401 — the dehydrated people, the first

few, asking for slake, shrivel and askew faced, look west.

3.

Squirrel fritters and climbs stalking when
filling his cheeks, burrows up and under this tree. Feet up to gravity,
Head to loves, no one will see him until after fall.

His slender climbed chicken wire of my window, screens to feast
body arrowed. His teeth edged from shells.
He and his well-rest, will want from hunger for months.

My extended family, me, played cards last summer.
Board games, cheesed slider potato salad plates.
Gulps and guffaws in the grass needles.

We sensed a season change in this humming
day. A niece's messy afropuff and frown: Some anchor on
her like, living. My ankles became full of welts, skin bubbles
'round feet. Engorged anklet. Mosquitoes flit, still feed.

(I rubbed alcohol, drip lotion and the itch left. It kept
coming back until it's breached.
Dem keloids blendin' in as we speak!)

Difficult hereditary straits on this country here.
Something out of this nunnery, this place, we made.
The blue jays' many calls are after

the orchard. Robin pushing with beak
red body and black wings in the coloring flora,
hard to see, secreting, she winks in my autumnal cooing sympathy.

(Anyway, "looka here: when you see my caul
see me, when you di'int, I see you." Oh baby.
Will water be wacky as canary eyes.)

We have these. We'd had. The birds on
rafters manage not to shit on each other. The piper
around pessimism is a whisper in peeping.

4.

Could those Dark people, moved, who
lived on in brokered strength
know what would buoy from their

bedraggling? The penalized, agile
muscular busters, as bucks with dick antlers? Through tense
and thistle of the sheened, stack corded mothers? People

of so-called intellect began, clipping into
the vast drink with knuckled hands, the children
of frailed Moors, and more. Sounds no

whipperstill for new natureland.
As persons who stubbornly head-butted through,
duressed, encapustuled, scurvied. Those of us form

the phalanx of kings, their scion. Profile of a few faces
lurching to the sunset of empire. I shake out of harkening, see
the tackling birds fight for my lineups of pre-seedling.

I wonder where they go
in quiet
when brambles and light are bare?

5.

They disperse as every one
memory I view them waiting
unexplanatorily for myself, put me here.

Today is falling new, they come back to some frosh, the air, year of seeing clearly
the whistles of claws, crossed their ways
a language echo I know, in our Black constructed first names.

Seasonings sift and things go back to
where they. The world turns spiraling bake,
shapes, sound small and unseen things, believe in sol's rising.

The sun shifts their minute shadows
when they shudder
so many scads of sparrows.

Correlation =/= Causation

For in-stance, this still tree here, I good luck knock saying hello.
Moving its frilled extensions up/down: this
isn't salutation from it only a small, flit, incisor
maybe be twix slip stream by town-
houses, waft in the back.

When one goes with to "step on
a crack, break your mother" it doesn't
in/occlude, pre-order concrete slabs,
placed on jack-hammer earth, only means
unintended rupture. Small roots have
inside(ous)-push to surface, to hug

Other things who exist at the expense of what made you:
progress or a job, pets and kids, .edu, domicile.
Some time things just show, like poems. We don't
know what to do. So we spec, think, plan, but do they
turn out?

Mind is tricky as are gut renovations. We wish what
we have always had gives new insight, sides, sighs. Make
sense of senses of
coincidence would mean variables of luck and un
luck: numbers, not saying
the play's name, in case the three shows up, riddling.

There's Always Time

Triceps, the harder muscle to tame, sinews the western gun.
Off-camera cackle rough as a lion's tongue. Oh correct killers
—oh weeping fury. I see sun sky colors and I hang

them around me. I walked the earth's corners, squaring myself in multitudes,
man's miasma, yet in love with each kaleidoscopic angle,
quilted triangulate patterning.

Tulip and eye, cultivars, "I see you as one
of the hopeful." My different-hue brother, dust of domain
in your visage, furrowed brow ridge. At the edge, the radial

moment, hot sun holds in the dermis of mine own. Encapsuled, D vita
min weak, where we've initiated. Ever unsated, outsize force, irises glum. Here
we gold banded be. Find ourselves, cold drying bend under iron ton,

as they said we aught: "learn, teach yourselves, our better ways." Uni, Gilead
balm, we dutifully recite cyrillic gestures, make do their dumplings, the particular
root beat stain, unifying hearts. Then the sp-sh-elling

At the razor check, small seam of certainty. The enemy isn't getting
out, someone sees, the day enough, within the deeps, caravans of fear rearing
bald tire huddle cries, huffing to breathe free, indistinct difference exhalating ()()

pause: to repeat, on our abattoir side, stutter, ellipses, tracks down the road,
easy to discern. Money crumbling, worth these bejeweled seconds to circle a
wrist, all the way up thin sleeves, fling us: a Mount Olympus disc,

Jesse Owens' forward toe, into the white, white, white snow
                              all our cousins, our kin reign on
us.

                                        (invasion, March 2022)

Griner Grounding

If she were he, if she were damsely,
if we coulda watched her tone, (fine muscle flex)

her stretch, retching wife, unseen.
If not for her, long limb, bright teeth

point 3: (ungowned) ball, gone in, let go? Her upswept long-dreading. Her digits tip-
bending (our Michaelangela, space of hers, time's ticking rim).

If she weren't so good, so great back, gaze-straight boned
blacker lashes, her complex so, bronze enough

for US to not Seal team slip plan, in to get sis gone. Instead wade, wait…
If she wasn't born strong, so strange for her to stand alone, stand, be out

no doubt, she'da *been* saved. Yes. The qweens—shout

(Pride month, 2022)

Eaten Alive

Bear Catches a Fish
(Something brings it back)
(Bishop sees the hooks)

Bear catches a fish
Polar, Black.
Piebald panda says *I ain't in it*

Bear catches a fish
wriggles in his mitt
was going against the current

Bear catches a fish
Doesn't care, liquid eyes
Doesn't care, what flitters necks

Bear catches a fish
Oh fish, bare(ly) says, *what else am I*
Going to eat? Takes one claw to open:

Little salty bubbles in fur
Red red bubbles in fur
Roe in this calus-hand. Roe in a calloused hand

Leviathan

i roe roe roe your boat
sa(i)d capt. ahab queeg
pinprick iris queues the great white—

full moon
naked in hotel bed
the soft pillows

moonlight slivers
blinds half open
red blinking time

white apron, black slacks
silently leaves
the paper outside

sun creeps under a shade
eyes fly open
plane's engine revs up

plastic room key, credit card
splayed, desk reserved
taxi mirror awaits

(linked senryu)

A Hip Hop Manager & Video Stylist Fly from LA to NYC

that one time I met June Ambrose

Bald Black, Nikes
Indigo hoodie:
Deep set eyes shining
The sky and see,
A self-made pair in the stars

Share a bitty bag full of mini-
Famous Amos choco-chips.
He cannot keep his lips
Away from the top
Of his wife's belly, his ear

'round her pouty areola.
He rubs her spine like
He's coaxing flame.
She let the sun work
Its way into her hair.

Curled copper crimps
Makeup-less, eye covers
Crimson shutter with pleasure.
They could get away
With this up here.

Sun patinated everywhere, this bubble
A kettle. An inviting spout
Where her 'innie' outs.
This fixed-to-the-hip,
striations of earth tones

gold filters through lashes,
the plane's shades, the dermis
pulsing. Twilight wraps the speck
of aircraft, pacifying.
Moving, moving to holy east.

winding road to the interiority

House Pent

NYC walkups, euphemism for "poor but proud." You gain light
but have to hike: groceries, laundry, the mail downstairs.
San Fran has hilly knobble streets: everybody's got great gams.
Here we try quadricep for days, weight bearing pelvises,
half lift two-fisted plastic shopping bags gravity and mass full.

You get the place when you're mid-20, the only spot left for
sans roommates. Hell, we're close enough together on the train,
hours every morning, millions of droopy-faces,
yet steely eyes in coffee cups brimming with bodega Bustelo.
(Name brand cafes to-go, for rube new locals out of our walking rhythm.)

In your formal 30s, you're glad for anything that makes you feel taut,
as if you had a run in. We walkups rarely get time to clear our heads:
gigging, hustling, arting, odd jobs, "consulting", staying on top of things
is the grind. Our cartilage surrounded by what fine-tunes balance as the steps
slope to our soles. The highest stairway cradles only us. Banister softened by our palms.

You haven't moved someplace better by now, don't leave 'til you must. It's only money.
Money's all there is. Not kids, lovers, spouses, elderly ones, pry you. They join you,
coming, then going. This is all you know. These walls, settled dust, its corners. Where
the linoleum and plaster pare. The trees push proximate outer masonry up, a spider seams
to you. You gain cred, the newcomers' sideways glances, irony.

You're on the other side of it now, you lean where it slides. Mutual crutch.
The landlord bribes you or breaks you. Usually the latter. Too run down to fight.
If you're tough lucky you kept the same lawyer for repairs, warmth, ceiling up, filled-in floor

gapes. If Grand Central Station's Mercury winks your way, they're getting so much refraction from glass box makers, they toss a few cubic zirconia shards your way, to cut out.

In either case, compromised, you go, lower, caterpillar razes bristles, entomb creaks, memories, where you climbed.

Corona of Thorns, Day of a Babe's Birth

The great building's antenna shrouded in puffs of slate
covered carousel horses and temporary fences
only a few early runners with pooping pups that had to be out, with me.

I haven't been to church since my patent leather mary-jane single digit days:
Once after school, learning, I ask why the god of love did those Job things?
the non-theologian part-time babysitter/church lady fumbles a non-answer.

My kid foundation cracks. There were other books, stories, worlds to know. Yet now on
drizzly days of meditation, I go back, as many of we isolates have, to small selves, the first
felt expanse of this realm's meaning, other tales to just reach.

Coulda sworn one night when I was eight, I heard sleigh bells.
In the projects, yes. Chimneyless. I woulda put my hand to little fluttering heart. I *knew*
goodness was rewarded, magic in earshot, around, hidden.

A reminiscent glistening on slick asphalt of the park. I think, *lágrimas alivias de Maria.*
Always a new day is born, we are something to salvage, through the bleak streaks.

Snapshot: Baby Bikini Et Al

1.

I flip to a rubber beach cap on my head with plastic flowers: Giant petals. Eyes irises in photo. Coney. Coney-Coney. Between toes, then cooler feet tops. Wind pick-ups. Blanket stripes wan sun, fried chicken, fruit and soda warm inside. Ice melts, thermos smelts.

Sun wasn't hot hot but still: The day was arranged. Nude tummy, beachballed by fat and carbonation. I snuggle under someone, dozing shade. Laid out lawn chair like, I'm in part shadow, withdrawn from moisture edge, polyblend land raft.

That too much feeling: No basketball or football play to this day, averting any rubber skin something, unforgiving tightness. I'd heard more than seen Sandy. In rem someone keying my door, haggard movements, dreaming.

2

Unseen, smaller than the pic. Hopping in & out of water, a bobbing red brown, skinny legs, golden laughing. Kid bro shares a birthdate with pre-us fam Ophelia, a hee-he who beach played 'til he played out, mother cousin vitiligo youngster foreshadowing his own mottling.

Some never leave the water. Long purples. RIP tide. A soul learns over lives. My man-now sibling, drops in after staple-sheet night-owling. The water rose from under house crawlspace, garlanding his wall borders as wood warped.

BK water-edge ramshack-framed dinghy bobbleheads. Geek computer grab, leaves to save self & circuits, linking to my wi-fi. He check-checks for weeks here, clicking, clinging to his worl(d)s. Now, I knew, I'm his home harbor for a grown sir version (big sis).

Sum. / 'Too Oh

oppressive June heat
whirrs near a window
lower helicopter

To Poem Inside Darkly

Hand-grasping, the branches
ends bud. Pustules of red along
the grey-brown bark.
The leaves are late, into the cruelest
month, only stems. They remind
me of Morticia in the show who used
to cut off bulbs admiring the sticks
and the perked pink thorns' tips.
Her slick black dress bottom fronds roots.
Her foreign lover, an amalgam of Latinates' tongue.
Is this tree from here? Is it a transplant from a ship
a gale pillowed to shore? Was there oak before?
Or is this ash? An ample tree in summer full of living blood.
Her squirrel squirrels a nest of discarded, crisp oil wraps.
Framed like this, here the weeping willow further 'way seems
to enjoy the absence of us breathing underneath.
It's small greens growing. Why not my arbor or its ivy? Am I to blame?
I talk to it through panes and it waits, for me to leave, but I don't.
Plague envelopes, my carbon, damask velvety cloak.

Exhaust

Droplets morse porcelain somewhere
in home. Too slouched to upturn I just
wonder, as it becomes scrim.

Aubade is abstract as is
the hyper-oxygenation that
usually contents nostrils around now.

I fear to even ajar the wind-
ow since what might wriggle unseen
in my broadband pupil, unearths more

about me than the outbreak. I'm executing
my best to look on the bright, but face
west and ever see beacons drain to murk.

5 Pieces of Advisce-ra: Memoria Meditations on Interior

1.

—even thinking about this my shadowed forefinger knuckle twitches

Everything's okay:
I consider it, still. To begin to know what words can do: bed-written kid.
Scribing in-space. All I need are "eyes." Where uttering starts, dissociate.
A super=power I suppose, like being able
To fall, sleep on cue: of use.

Imagination expanded like a Charlie X's. (my irises roil back.)

Blurring tv yet mostly, closed. I dreamt, I imaged writing.
In a sealy twin, maybe full. Green felt, wrapt up.
Window at the back of my skull.
Airing, at solstices I see a weeping willow without, turning.
Something *sssshhhhh* the leaves, bowed branches

I see its colors. How? What's behind that kind of sight?

Cranium fits on the spine socket, all the way, up (in) there.
My mind's optic nerve perched at the tree, in and above a pillow.
I write this way, still: I have something
on my mind, in mind.
Seeing what isn't what I had "off the top."

2.

Hard to pencil in that lay(er)ing time. Words? *Hmph.* What I can say is I carry this piece
(maybe for luck) always with me. I wouldn't let that go, that weeping, the hue's murmur
it made. Green sleeves, springshade. There are parts of me, there are parts of you,
parts of shifted trees, coral and birds we tuck in "past." They are in a locket.
I open it and it makes me wrested.

I try to place it—

3.

I was blue _____there was nothing
I could do. Then I felt it
was Fortuna. To not lose one
        's mind but to loose it
it's anchor, you know? Oh! kedge
        dredge what's up
In this trial, this seering mark,
        hidden in the back.
Ahead, I saw myself walking from that bed,
passed the plastic accordion door popular of the time,
akin to shimmery beaded curtains, blood lacquer pseudo-Sino screens
dividing rooms, thick hot slip
covers. I knew I'd go down the stairs into the open out-doors.
I dreamt myself falling but happily, my limbs
flailing. Inside I felt at a piece.

4.

When you have no thing left to do, you can sit with things. Half a lung away. I lay down
With tinny percussion ticks going around the inner gateway of the room. I read and
read, catching a breath. Pulmonary bends, the rest of me.
Pain is a roommate you're used to. You two develop a sketch.

Death is a wink, an aside, an opinion. Moiling, the slushing of Life Is *sweet, so sweet.*

Everything in hums with it, brio, teeming, a soft rattle. That sound tinkles, tickles
the toy of a babe. I sense its shadow then, now: I walked through such gapings
following it, leading it. One day, one day, some ever point. Yet this Honey is still
in my tongue, nerves, the sibilants.

5.

A Prayer: May the clatter one day be *soft, soft, soft*. May the tree's branches glaze my countenance, veil me. May the touch be so far, I cannot imagine it's feeling, everything inside my self is surprised, says *ssssshhhh*. You've earned this lovely bed.

No time high noon, none, I supplicate now. I can see, at any point, then.
Pronto, I savor Body's iron on the back of my slang,
where the throrax meets it, and says
parallels the spine, it's liquid.

In the new cen, I cannot move again, become a custom to treasure *little inklings*.

Prism

1.

How did we get here?
How do we go, Black?

We like heat, sun colors epicarp

Grey mottling sea, don't we know
how the water's sheen dissolves

skin breaks skin down.

Inside blood is not the superficial hue
hydroxygen, eyes decide

everything we know refracts colors, are not.

2.

God, if you are somewhere, you have abundance—so many
names—does mine come through? Hours?

When we say any—those calls together—
how'd they holed up? Does it echo? Feel like a shaking hand?

Wind tremors, as it carries
our after-silence

What's close enough to Black fading?
What's farthest?

Searing, blinding light sends color back, millions shard
Cold Black, coal occluding, concludes. They're together.

Pinprick eyes, teeth lined,
half moon gleans full flesh

Open, stutter, aperture tap
twinkle light fire, heaven, permamap

striped dermis, layer all the way to porous white, all the way to charc, all
the way to ash.

Oh corpus, your primary colors known.
Hover, cover, pelt, cutis, clot, new sin, bone.

Steel Away

(lyrics)

Working day and days,
all-iron in my blood now
Shackles on my hands, my brain
They say I'm free but how?

I hammer down the line,
folks said I done wrong
Chinese man on the other side,
different words in the same song

Chorus:
Farther away from home
Neither one can get back
Chattered teeth, clanging bone
We bang out more tracks

John Henry whispers to me
Says he shouldn't have beat that drill
Story makes us proud to be
Worked to death by free will

Iron, carbon make steel
Body of the guitar you play
Shoulder business' grinding wheels
Ashes, fret lines to my last days.

hymn, hum

Araminta

1. One step forward

Scrambling fingers
rough hewn nails
dirt and microscopic moss

creek stones slip
ankle twist
it blooms

cotton drags at hem
a tawny string
matches the edge

hair brambled twigged
she seems like landscape
huddling sunset cooling

no teeth, no smile—yet
stomach like bark
hollow parts blood coursing

the fork is up, yes.
large flat leaves
skittering things

a flat farm
high grass perimeter
expectant harvesting

2. Two steps

So soft her spring
Born Araminta. Our Perseph
Evergreen and night kin

She ages in cool cloth, throned
recalls the brackish, sharp air
her own mother, birthing variations of herself,

Wedded to living death, eating fruit
mushrooms twixt cadaver blades
avoiding the slick

Once and once again
that hunger, that desire.
dandelion on hand, for wishes

she takes the time to count
each spun off in the breeze
says: "that many."

Aminata: Daguerrotype

her fingers, ivy covered
gestures the hither sign
the same flexion at her hip

so lovely, ember eyes
steel heating there like her back
don't flinch says *mother to son*

daughter of eve says "the Lord
made light" and me, the truth
each follow the beam, burnished sight.

African Things Seen

We African things
made to thing
Not people, things
Not worked to death b/c things, ka-ching
not raped because, things (any hole, a goat)
the discreteness of things
(no thing from miles around, an aching thing sound)

Existential Rooster, Paul D. says: they cradle
 his scion, the eggs gently until they are out
—of sign of the hen
His yoke is ochre: blood, the sun, rust?
The block chain here comes from something else
but is it really? Want to hear a grimm plumage for true?
Statuesque isn't an "esque" if she's not a she but some (thing) mess.

"Made me feel pretty good" says the Black man on the DNA selling test.
"I didn't know I had some Irish in me…" says he. Some great, great.
How double (duboisian dc) can you get? How CG Woodson is you?
(Were you watching retro Danny Kaye (passing as) and got swept up in the melodics?
He, adorable as hans, christian cos to be sure, rockin' flame tresses like Kirk D,
you ain't neither of hims, of he.) Nether regions of "not she.": A crew of somebodies,
white bonafides, from their "ends" to her bad spot in, at the end of.

"____ she was taken." was how my great uncle succinct, said it. no ellipses. *dassit.*
she, limp back ballooned. and was held. we "she'd" her. we, we she'd her tears.
and he'd the newbie, the babes and babes were bathed and babbled! they splashed
in amniotic waves. they splashed in a heavy tinned tub, they guffawed

in a kiddie pool. they wore (fallo) tube tops and got soaked by the johnny pump
they went to coney island and jumped up and down in water and salt. they planed their first
trip back and heart-healed. they went down the Nile because Old (School) Kingdom roots

starts south, like the great rivers we know, and reap, repaired, floating at giant Black Memnon
sentinental look looking and looking. saw unremarkability in Egypt and of Wolof.
I re(as)semble Moor-i-tanian in Daker, *cousin*. Someone in Cairo's profile is my brother's.
Natural Malcolm color coils of many Ghanians (so-called deficiency for them, knot for
Northern kin). My hair wrap in Casablanca makes me wholly similar, as per the hagglers
who look to me, then the translator, quizzically.

Whenever someone asks me a "mixed query" I know the economy

is unfiltered white, no matter where. I get it: the whole world but I mean
right there. No matter the color, my hue being is amalgam but not when some color-run ish:
variation on a double-helix theme, not metaphor. How many different "bantus"? A hole world.
A whole
subset: a pinhole kaleidoscopic sapien sapiens prowess. Knowledge bringers crack spirals
unwound de-wound melanocentric code. It's not pallor of white reverie, display; it's
unblemishment of anything in high relief.

"Black Jesus" (redundancy) is only joking for non-Black people. We like just saying Black
sometimes. Only two things we have to do, you see. [insert wisdom here 'bout being free]
The sans sunscreen Max von Sydow apogee in the heat, the deserting, would have been
written as His magicianship. (Not listed.) Racio-Biblio do-over unscript cottony coils two helix
to flaxen snow. Color wine to water, full-bodied impossible, burnished brass to alabast, a
palimpsest. You look up to who reinforces you: logical, devotion to. We see Buddha's wrapped
knots in Flatbush, peaked hair, depending on the where, facial variations, his universal tummy.

Black feng shui: Malcolm X and baguas: Knowing where the door is, your back to the wall
facing it. A Detroit spatial awareness. A Brooklyn cunning, a Chicago understanding, an LA
frontier foreshadowing.

The spirit of an uninterrupted field with a lone tree

Not an ancestral ring (shout) round rosy baobab. A sturdy maladaption, our rendition of the one Odin was flipped on. His hands releasing runes, our cultures' global splay: versions of lines in Hair that *leys*. S(tr)ange/sangre/shange/saged/coagulate weeping sap merge beautiful w blood, tree bark, the brown greyed. What waves in windless day? Us? A flag flag(eolet)? Who who? A black bird?

Also often thinged but still. Black wholly.

Kenning-Beginning[*]

> "In the beginning was the Word, and the Word
> was with God, and the Word was God."
> —John 1:1 KJB

> "…b/l/oh/w win(ds)… b/l/oh!"
> —*King Lear*, Act 3, Scene 2, William Shakespeare

…Oh God (a. coltrane's sun in-tones)
Oh God (says one coming)

Oh God (sans "o", they mean (it).
You? Breath-omni? little-chest?)

"O" in Oh & "o" in G-d sans O is one-tone.
Yes it sames. You, tin-eared.

Oh, 1st sound: joy, (at)las/t, knowing: globe-tone.
O, 15th note, circle mouth-wonder, disdain, vague, su(r)prise.

ZerOh. Mouth-pivot. 3 skin layers circle-letters. dank-down-dark
Dermises bronzing curlicue black dot, fine-print it.

Your clay-made hearing, you, newly-born. Your ear can't-ear like cat's year.
You, Bas/t earshot-jealous: feline-twitches, no-need-turning.

Punto. What do I do? Drive them circles so they dust.
They will, Sirocco, scour. Sands. r/h/ound. Ent(r)ails.

---

* in appreciation of Ishmael Reed's "I Am a Cowboy in the Boat of Ra"

61

(I see: orbs
what/t/'s inside.)

My will is my in/ten/t. It's g - - d. It is firmament-made. Its-firm.
The hole of me is not-me. Its-all. Oh-ve(e)r. And this is why I will win(d).

Calving, Halving: Wails to Sinai Moses

Glit. Go?
Be without you? Where could we

Primary cast? Where would we, woodless?
Oh eruptors of man's compelled ora—

Death. The bone of man's de/cisors.
It, pliable and hardens, like silt and sand

Of deep mines, volcanic lustre.
Conscentcration. Oh concent consequence

Glows. Oh ember of earth/fire's
Shine don't glisten but

So many (in)scribe, in it, purity.
Burnished tint, tarnished ash, glint.

Arwald The King

The last free Wight man lives with me. I'm nomading the earth's face, never
comfortable sediment, sand at the edge of the deep sea, its breach.

Cutter craft jumps from Jersey to Guernsey to Wight. Prosaic, picking up a tote, too
heavy a swivel-case. I land following footsteps. A dark man, player king who'd shift
mass and archipelagoes, dying a foreigner ages before my birth.

I find myself as he was, the sole Black person in this whole small plot. I find myself
soon—holding my chest, treading to this unbeknownst summon, as ancient
chorus:

At the dock the shadow of a tree is flat on a bleached building in isle. The small
trolley, trundles to a tiny residential museum, someone's place, a legacy, whom I
didn't know. This little tract guides me to wander, custom out of place.

Why does my clavicle heave now? Unusually heartsore by the small excavation, crypt
diorama of the way back then. Grief for Arwald. One who, like mine own, recalls

whom his ancestors idolized. Combat cries curdle blood-sodden ground made hard
mud I tip- toe, tracing. Romans see over and over come to lower him in penance.
They bring salvation, kill power—he knew—their sanguination pyre in Wight's
new wounds.

Arwald keeps supplicate and with the sword. King, I got close to sobs, Phantasm, yore
prowess, still radiates this grave-size haven.

My self's center feels heaviness of your veins, these chambers. The room within
rhizome of red corpuscle, the oxygenating breeze, this turf of echolocation in artery.
Memory tends to reverb- walls. Your unheard sounds shake my upper trunk.

Now in my bit of house, in a borough jotting, my eyes fringe your resound
   piety, you're uttering: "My God, more than my person." Your knowing cloaks
   thews as all

the knives pierce you together.

The last thing you see, as endemic protoplasm embeds stone, who's carrying off
   your sister, her name unknown. She, Persephone of Wight, womb of their
   first

dynasty.   Yes. I shudder at this too, Arwald. Centuries of my myriad
   mothers know her wails.

The Dawning of the Age, the Spheres

1.

Nobody said it would be easy, when it comes
The crescent is a sickle, a scythe, edges things
for the universe is round, borders don't define
ends. That is just, the way things run. A whole, an outskirt

a cusp. I see this slip of Mother Earth's suckler, part of this
on its own. Like all children it's slipping from Terra, Mama, self-making.
Hope once it pulls back it'll outlive where it's from.
No longer our umbra, our dust.

Glitter half-ring pulls me in: how far to touch
in this room, w*(h)*ere I can't go. Tuxedo cat stretches on glass.
I wonder how those markings, one bouncing off all rays, the other
albinism, a cover and an underbelly.

That moon is like so, drawing up, dawning. The edge, the whole, sometimes no
thing. Shadows of electric light. What gives? I should not be able to see
my African statue outline, discreet sentinel. My eyes—
were made for this system of slight light, emerging as blaze's day. Shift-shape.

2.

In the heat and constructed billow of harnessed lightening a device moves air,
pips when it self-sleeps. This may be when the last of these luxuries skitters
off. This may be when only open windows, candlelight cats'
eyes pierce movements, still outlines. McCoo

Davis, LaRue, Townsend, McLemore presaged our number. In the Fifth we will again be
left to devices; we've eaten all the ever-expanding decaying tree of knowing.
A woodpecker's stripes red, black and white making holes for light, reflects
or initiated. Cosmos-time doesn't mean things aren't supposed to happen, don't.

Yet lodestars. *Hair* was Broadway, some of us sprinkle in,
this Dogon-descended quintet sound wholesome Black psychedelia
aspirational anthem against anathema. Ogotemmêli in their woos, aspirational and blue.
Billy's growl sparks, the sun's system, permeates our Delphic chak…

A choir entices holy notes, herald juncture of cut-out dross, our five ring circles,
we beam.

The First Brother Arrives

The orbs are completely black as if we'd seen a ghost, as if someone dilated hollowed-out bone. Something to be said for this, that rider, the horses we were then landed here, the steeds with grey metal men on them, tinny claiming godhead.

He didn't blink for a while taking in the hole sun, stilling his calloused undergirding. Sour smell never to leave pickled skin.

Perversely, no rust in their over-bent joints. Good as new, as fresh water. When they were iron-walked, it was as if a mirage, so accustomed to the salt's bite. No aftertaste? How many months, eons had it been?

He wobbled tenterhooks, they'd say. Landlubber, he was tall for his age, hardly loved anyone off the shared tit. Almost age enough to be initiate, remade.

—

The best teeth, the best gums. A foreskin cut too deep after. Heaven sees him, the songs say, once he catches the tune.

He/they made their own current, eventually it became a whistle, a slide, a lingo, a stride.

—

Sometimes you have to make up your mind.

previously

Invisible Man on a Station in the Metro

I'm Specter—between underground stations. I used to know them a little and they knew me. I was eating with them sometimes. We would exchange phrases.

One day, my self began making cameos. It happened while I was eating grits and once again in a public place. I felt *dis/em/bodies* 'cause, I had been a shell of my origin for such a long time.

It felt like gelatin in the beginning. (I don't eat that stuff—cloven hooves.) But this is how it seemed at first. It began to expand like a marshmallow: It was good it felt overly sweet. I began to ask myself—is this a guilty pleasure?

....

One day, it happened. It wasn't just a resident; it was me. Filling up cubby holes in my bones, and I did not feel bloated!

I was doing so much better before. I had friends I could gab to about clothes & political goings on. Anything that didn't require commitment. I began to say less, telling more. I was not the hydrogen everyone says I am now.

Truth is, I began to thin out. To them, turning translucent. More corporal cause they noticed, less real because my guts began to show in high relief. No one wanted to watch that.

I saw they began to move slower, stiller life. Sure, they were picnicking between the openings of the tracks at Grand Central. Yes, they had wicker baskets, sandwiches with some meat, and red drinks and chips. I wanted to sit with some of them, especially exotic looking types, touring. When I tried to rest for a moment they would not hear me say hello. They saw condensation on the can, soothing sounds of my throat and they clinked their glasses!

I even moved on to strangers I barely knew. Crossed some invisible line, protocol and they wouldn't hear me or speak.
Now this hurt me. I could understand taking sides, but I faced these people frontways. There were no sides to take!

I move on between the numbers, glance at the board, sit by myself. Unpack, look at my feet, hoping they're still on the ground. Withdraw (oh, pen!)—I know I have to get this down.

Tragedies in Acts: Avoiding Emmett Till at Furious Flower's Blacksonian

In Accra, Mom wanted to go North where
the tallest Ghanians abide, Othello-like,

we'd sojourn, weirdly combine, daughter crone, recall bleak magic, sail ships docks.
I instead advocate for tilapia so fresh we remain lounging south by Tetakwashi Roundabout.

I lie then. Now before this black tie thing, neck time thing, I stop by the bottom rim
of DC's upside down triangle, quiver hitting home, ere prepping aesthetics to perform.

African (Am) Anubic land, I walk under earth, saw roots of that poetic day, taction muffled
breath, feet shuffles from one cased ampere to the next.

Heavy aerating hvac, I emerge earth-level, furthest I could go.
Time to gown for a ball, taffeta covers, a pregnant pause, over pine, eternal hold, pleats

avert an aortic rupture source, promising to return to that thresh, that last square.
He waits. Dakar dead do. Crypt above Accra. Across Congo saying "come."

There are things I can't. I celebrate beings brave. I looked askew at the cliff door, Sunu Gaal
from sea shored. I could have been Black Gertrude this day report this innocent babe, puffed

fore, head garlanded by nettle, how our
cracked crania could repeat inner swells erupting cheeks.

I fear upheaving grief. I've bowed to Dubois' tomb, other great warriors who've won.
At the sparkling display, I cower above the frown of Mamie's murdered son.

How Many Crows Does It Take to Make a Murder?

After Duriel E. Harris' "He Who Fights with Monsters"
for Kerry James Marshall and Raymond Patterson

How many black birds along a tree?
How many blacks on a tree?
How many on a tree?

How many backs to a tree?
How many backs like a tree?
How many blackened trees?

How much coal? How many caws on the tree's top?
How many cauls along branches?
(How many trees?)

How many leaves?
How do the blacks leave?
How many flee?

How many hearts up a sleeve?
How many black black strings across?
So so many. So so so many, many.

cubby

a   part
a   pod
two   peas
to play,
tutus.   Sweet—
as icing   Sweet—
Bird songs in the park.

Mom   and   Dad
Are   keen   to some—
things: Gestures
tell-tale   faces…

In the dark,   quiet
humming   room
we   came
to   know
(there will always be whispers no one else can hear)

Sookie Now: Pam

1.

Miss thing strolling in clingy culottes, platforms, tube top.
Hair braided back to two 'fro puffs.

We was like: *chp*. "She *thank* she cute!" Loud enough
For ourselves, cheap snack passing, for food.

Me an' my fren' 'cross the street, (cause gossipee's
a ass-kicker. Harder in heels)

The boys down the block lean away from her, bouncing
Their heads to her bootie as she moves past weak cat calls.

2.

Green uniforms matching the garbage bags, big as them,
Detritus: Piled corpses for pick-up. Say things

Young ladies shouldn't hear from men who resemble
Their fathers. Spectors take two hours to do a fifteen minute job.

Keeps her same game face from the low rent high rise to the minimum-wage job at the big
white wall street bank.

Snap

A breakup in the concrete, your mother's back.
Residue from switches, birch skin, falls:
A fingershell in the city's leprotic air.

Around the buildings, skyscraped apt houses
Between chain ringlets, the sun is small, white
Relentless summer's thumbnail sketch.

The suspension of fiery rubber, an orange ball.
Responds to black tarp, wan concrete base around
The park borders.

The edge and the action, vaselined, kindling, we
Look out at the gamine, the unforgiving surface on
Which we stand.

What's a snap? Moving our necks side to side.
Heads west, corners of smiles tucked easterly.
In our cornea circles, the turned around image burns.

For The Woman's Pearl

i

first the bug falls after
skimming the curled lip.
softness is the secreted life.

a dream, dream.
chelate, chitin;
tangible as teeth.

ii

(how would *you* feel if somebody
abraded your plaque looking
for yellows as gold?)

iii

i'm so good at making something out
of mistakes, i pay for this over and
over.

what do i get out of this deal
before i'm shucked and jived?
never ever ending work.

(Museum of Natural History
Pearl Exhibit, New York, 2/2002)

Around the House

The tube sock with the red and green stripe
is missing its partner. Red and blue, black and blue.

White white drawers, tee-shirts—Too much bleach
in them. My cousin has problems. He scratches

his legs like his mother treats her face. Vociferously,
sometimes using the teeth

of a comb. A hard brush. Bright sweat socks,
with correct, alternating stripes, determined

from a block away, due to the flat-rolled Levi on the left.
But if you played ball—like my cousin did when he could

get out of his room—you had to have both sides rolled.
The sweat aggravating the Clorox in his calves' pores.

Gramma understood, in that Bill Withers way,
him. The crying. The sneaking suspicion around

him. What he had about himself. Bummy clothes
when he went to school and silk shirts to put on

in his dirty bag. They had a chemistry, them two. She
on the top floor, he in the basement with the clothes.

* * *

I'm a gnat lighting toward Burt Ward: BLAM! The door
slams. Was it a brush, a chair, a belt, a rolled towel?

Gloves are missing partners, as every winter.
Left hand goes into a pocket—it's back in the day:

Cool has another new look. Frost bit tips around
a nickel bag—a holey pea-coat pocket. A hip dips.

walking the block. Keloids under corduroy, nylon
mock-neck sweaters. A skull-cap
twisted tight, a plate on the head.

If I didn't want to eat something,
like meat, at Gramma's, all

I'd have to say was that a fly landed on it.
My grandma didn't have roaches, ever

but with the window open, the big cooking
all year... She was vigilant. Two steady eyes

for their dozens. A speck on the big mirror in her bedroom
wasn't dried lotion, hair pomade, leftover perfume spritz

it was them: and how on earth she could even identify tiny
fly poop was a mystery like her yummy hoe-cakes

and fine hair, her American Indian face. "Don't pout
your lips out. That's why they're so big. Keep them

tucked in." She says. She uses less lipstick than
anyone in that house. A tube would last—years.

* * *

Me, now? Tops: Three months. I am not neat. I don't
cook a lot unless someone is invited in — to my house.

Banging pots. My mirrors are dusted
with fog from the World Trade Center.

No kids. Cats quieter than mice. No
pests of any type. Gramma used

to clean on the side for her own going-out-money.
Chat with her girlfriends, cuter than Coretta,

ever. (Now always, reposed in memoriam.) My grandfather
caught her with a mop outside and knew. He didn't let his wife

work for white folks period or work at all. They were "free" and not South.
Sweeping away, *rinching* dishes, watching kids.

For dressing up, cigarettes, a clutch for dancing.
Her fifteen kids (Grampa's and hers). She

was not the lady and the shoe. Her kids cleaned,
too. My mother still wonders where my recessive

messy gene is from. My lips are bigger than either
of theirs. I'm shorter. Talk more. Wear stockings with

sneakers to work. Do not have the scars like my cousin.
Grampa, silent mostly, kindly. An old-fashioned nudie

calendar after he lived alone, dying. The Grands broke up,
after his kids came to her door. After she let them stay,

and he had to go to the other house he owned. Spartan
but for pinups and boxes of old unopened gifts. Southerner

alone since twelve. Cut pelts for the rich.
Knew beautiful women and furs. Knew what softness was . . .

The big dog, my uncle's at the house, never got
Gramp's scents. Tried to attack him. He still stopped by Gramma's—

carefully. She still took care.
The Lord's day: she cooked hominy

and chops, smothered onions, eggs, cheese,
pan bread, coffee. Day's dishes cleaned before the last plate

was scraped. Cuz gained weight since I saw him last.
Smooth ebony skin above the neck. No hard feelings.

Medusa Oblongata Dread

sinewy sass snakeskin slink seamless spine
routed—out her head. helix exlixers, elicit, fine

ripple through time. so striking, blindin',
dem men turn to stone when dey admirin'.

An Unheard-of Blues

Silence ain't golden when you have abated breath
Quiet don't feel golden when you feel an unbreathed breath
Worser when you know the air ain't coming from yourself.

Last night I heard you sneakin', a spider up the steps
Caught in your web so sticky like spiders spinning threads
In bed put your arms 'round me, a cocoon, cold like death.

Creep is such a simple word, means so many heavy things
I mean creepy, you define that word. Can mean so many things
The wind brings your name up, "Creep" summon everything.

Postcard of Parmigianino's Self-portrait in a Convex Mirror

The postcard is about the curve, the hand, malleability. The hand is a mirror to the face, the face is a reflection of the glass. The glass is an eye, a fishbowl. A fishbowl I think strangulation. I mean, how far can you move your neck? In the classic, the convex is a collar. It is the noose of goodness, news of youth.

The postcard is like lynching ones in Atlanta. The postcard rings a southern bell. The southern belle is hot aristocracy, wears mediaeval clothes in sweltering heat. The band of sweat is hidden by the hand. The arm? The crook of the arm is the pen. The blot on the back is a Rorschach's test. What do you see in this glass? Look 'round.

He Used to Kiss My Hand

for Allen Ginsberg (2000)

Oh, Allen, now, after your death I finally look at you working, under my current age, in school after you left school, funny. After the shows, the floral arrangements at St. Ann's after reading Poe together, I see your notes. You read "The Bells" and I think of LL. I sang *Dream within a Dream* and who'd know you'd become one right after? We pay tolls to get from one stop to the other. We wish for stars and not to become them. Wanting to always touch and be.

I.

After your tie and glasses, neat male pattern, pate cranium, circumscribed by the ears. Your teachers hip at Brooklyn College and Columbia U (this is beyond irony, it is). In death, I call you familiarly, first name, chuckle. Now that our paths cannot cross, your trail.

And it was fun to see you in the mirror, camera turned to the side to see your other half, you in silhouette, profiling for me clip, clip at the type, writerly way. And this is what we have in common only (not really), besides our affection for Amiri LeRoi's Baraka Jones.

Icons of mine are not ologies but ials, optimism. You weren't a 50s Cleaver (neither Eldridge or Wally) but someone i.d.ed. I make all my OGs Rakim, (mos def). Should we lie for a poem? We should half-truth/double negative together. Exaggerating in the name of _____. Salvation? 2nd coming?

II.

It is not the North Star binding us, the heavens twinning. Both from the month of heat and flowers. Your birth's earlier but bound by hands, I declare. Every time we read/wed you would take my hand and kiss the back. You know, being /my/ kind, and would like that. With Jazz and (Hip Hop—that's for me) and bagels: don't forget Bob K (as if).

How do you, Hum, cosmol? Diamond crystals on Sun Ra's ship. Stars rules shoulders, talking thinking, doubles *y dedos*. Get done/down. Generefractions. How do I get it all in, like you? Ticking off each thing, conflagrations, thee are not simply your lists, there are still wars. Your prescient self: Nixon in this poem and in the barrage the silence of that go-to cat in San Fran. Not Ted's not yet.

My gen's mind not as eager as yours to eat from the garden of good & eve. Force fed McD's, Victorian secret bodies, Larry's lust and Craig's meet marketing. Refinement of conscription at the watery gate. Drowning in vertisments, words from the same place. Samesamesane, from all the spots, sound bites: no diffdiff-stiff. One plusone equal(s) won (but not us).

III.

I wish we had God to call. Wish we had angles, clear trajectories. I wish we could trust plaines, logic commonsense. I wish there was a synthesis right (now). We are not in the Aquarian age you'd be hopping to hear and be here. Just airy twins everywhere. That cold, hard element. We are not a blend, multiple states revolving, un(de)solving, de-stasis, stilted, omni-direct motion. The Cabbalists intoning now: tree of life is stumped, staying ohm.

Brazilian foliage is a long lawn, and speaking of bored, all the names became curses. Imitating, invoking. Martyrdom done neon. Shallow breathing, against ozone. Suntan lotion on the ears of albino kangaroos watership downunder. Portal to hell, I think: deceptive spherical as a heaven's body.

Feeling feline, AG, sitting on your papers, purring. Your bray here, stubborn Sirius. Bray the moon, pray & pray.

Canon Cannon Memoria

I don't know about you

In '59 I was

Checkin out across the sky

northern lights from the heavens colors every few

Red Green yellow purple, blue eyes. Shimmer glimmeri

miles

New Orleans so called jazz
cut my teeth big
swing Dix

My take bee Dizzy And miles
!
Cliff, Max kickin ass. Brown
vs board

little rock in arms. the Cold a shiver

that bomb!
Kind of Blue, '59, blew
cool uncool. hip and un.
spirit not act, true yesterday, still true

threads,

Ravel, Debus . Twelve-tone

without a score, stroll the studio, Chambers, Evans, Miles
trumpet, great John canon ball Philly drums.

The mood coo

Reflect a better way of it. Or another way
Miles over the group

a minor and sharp. Play the change.

bass, a 2 step. A soft shoe.

out taps. booty. cool

Sputnik floating earth. northern lights Birdland, Billie Lester
young. pads, LPs.

Earth from Mars. No Hollywood, no poets,

nor philoso or political scient,
intellectuals, always late

the music

.

All Blue,

I saw someone dance to Kind of. .

Flamenco

can you feel ? your pulse to

make it mean what you want it .

don't be j-i-v-e

with your
story.

!
The
Vanguard. The anti war replaced by LBJ. Martin Luther king was while Malco m .

Cronkite the days of "Cuba si, Yankee no".

In the midst of this, I found myself

" his last night!". I "Holy !" hurried my butt over

Miles, looking Cecily . "

Say miles! did you play   blue?!"

Didn't you hear ?"
recorded for the record. Miles

putting me on.
!!!!!!!

Feeling Brought In: Sketching Flexing, Fluxus, Flexibility and Afrofuturist Seeing of Dick Higgins

Hippies, Hipness, Jazz and Black culture
Stein strides, Langston and Higgins
Paik and the undeniable non-Whiteness of Being (post-War America)
Moorman and the female body eyeing areola of Higgins
Jay DeFeo's flowering and Higgins
Kinda Blue Higgins
What you hear is not a test: The State of Black Existentialism, "Steal this Turntable" and
    Dick Higgins
Don't be a Dick Higgins: Black aspirationality, safe exceptionalism and afro-anti-avant garde
    fear with Dick Higgins
Cecil Taylor's running commentary and multi-hyphenation with Dick Higgins
Code-switching and Luba memory boards and Dick Higgins' ephemera
Notation, bata and the intangible changing same already told Dick Higgins
J.A. Rogers autodidactic truth and the alternative knowing of Dick Higgins
Dick Tracy's watch, the non-status, panopticon stature of Dick Higgins
You don't know what it's got 'till it's gone, Tracie Morris being introduced to Dick Higgins

Mention Sarah Vaughan collab.
His mention of work songs that lead to jazz and nonsense. I mention glossolalia and Jay
    Hawkins. (a spell a spelling)

mention schwitters and the german references he has here.

m: "phatic" poems on p. 316 and reference "phatic acts" of JL Austin

m: phatic in the context of meaning of tm sound poetry
m: 317—mention of beats being heavily influenced by jazz
m: 318—any text that is not understood as words by the listener is a sound poem

m: 319—sound poetry in service to another medium (where something else takes place) like radio *plays*

m: 320—sound poetry is not music.

there is more to do with sound poetry

Characteristic Black Affect Philosophizers:

mimetic—field hollers (unnamed and misnamed enslaved)
mimetic modern—screaming Jay Hawkins and Nina Simone
Pragmatic—Prince
Expression—dissonant dub djs prototype of the sly and robbie phenom
Objective: sundiata's the philosophy of the cool
exemplicative: Kendrick Lamar, Jean Grae

Prep for Sarah Vaughan

m: "phatic" poems on p. 316 and reference "phatic acts" of JL Austin
m: phatic in the context of meaning of tm sound poetry
m: 317—mention of beats being heavily influenced by jazz
m: 318—any text that is not understood as words by the listener is a sound poem
m: 319—sound poetry in service to another medium (where something else takes place) like radio plays

m: 320—sound poetry is not music

Characteristic critics Modern:
mimetic: D'Angelo
Pragmatic: Ella Fitzgerald, Mahalia Jackson, Babs Gonzales
Expressive: Billie Holiday, Macy Gray
Objective: Sammy Davis Jr., Paul Robeson, Stevie Wonder
Exemplicative: Erykah Badu, Wangechi Mutu, Glenn Ligon, John Akomfrah

Ears, Nose, Throat, Rose: Seven Years' Last Breath

so slight is the thin bone between senses, silent air
respire broadens moving forward. in enough variety phrenologists comment
expulgated, leaving, it trails closer to the muscles furrowed over the bone above,
its intent. how many slightly nasal black boys sound like michael?
him so slight. the vitiligo showing his veins. so blue in that relief.

Sweat running off huge kid orbs in a huff,
pound cap over fro.

imagine that creole kid up north looking at him turn, looking at him turn.
alone shuttling from room to room, house to house, worming through a mini apple.
merged at big eyes, falsettos, tenors, hard fathers that make them burn, stars.
such pretty boys then men (then) that sound like chirping sparrows, hearts beating in their
    encased little breasts.

2016 Requiescat Break

Spring Prince
curls in "the elevator"
4Cs

lastly

The Occasions: Zhuitsu Wonder

After dinner and the dishes, we lounge from dining room table to couch and armchair.
My family speaks to inanimate objects to make music sound on. We hear the same tunes all
year, notes reassuringly reverb.

This, dangerous time for recall: Our favorite soul songs move the aftershock
of murdered men, one by one this country's medicative balm scoured. Contractions dismayed
hippies from their curdled ideas: Manson's evil twist, inflation, heroin targeting children
where the Panthers fed them, disintegrated.

Babies die before they're born, infected by the grief.

The non-aligned movement turned into inflationary global policy. The Crook's do-over after
his victor's head sheared, his Muslim confronting analogist destroyed by the preamble to the
force that feared Hampton's outreach in Appalachia.

Evil, why have you destroyed, you've destroyed so much of this doggone world . . . Evil

Circa the 200th of a fragile idea. This implosion of disappointment refashioned Marvin,
Stevie, Lennon, Labelle, Jimi, Prince, Croce, Wendy Carlos, Reddy, Santana, Pryor, P-Funk,
Carly, Rufus/Chaka, Carlin, The Temps, Janis Ian, EWF, Sly, James Brown

You can feel it all over, you can feel it all over, people.

emerging Disco and Hip Hop too. The hammer, stars, stripes and sickle responses framed in
our post-trauma china cabinets with Martin, John and Bobby memoria. Those times took
a toll on creators, creations, us. we each said *Mercy, Mercy...*

This world is moving much too fast, we're race babbling . . .

Socio-cultural movements, cultivated from post-WW2, when those little kids had kids. Our 70s were Ma's and Gramma's 40s through 60s on 78 and 33 rpms, our reel-to-reels, 8-tracks, boomboxes.

From the park I hear rhythms/Marley's hot on the box
Tonight there will be a party/On the corner at the end of the block

In the 80s the master blasters were made writ small to fit in our Reagan individualism (Walkman, male and singular). as did the violent responses to them. We suckled on that conflation of toxicants from then on.

Did I say Stevie? Always say Stevie.

Here I am baby (signed, sealed, delivered, I'm yours)

In Old San Juan, just settled in after two-hour coach, buzzing to be there. We all crashed the couch as if we were college roommates for a few days in the loft Airbnb. Everything felt palpable as the coming of age roots hang out with Nuyoricans

Es una historia que [el] amor reinará
Por nuestro mundo

like Pedro P. and esp. Miguel A. in Loisaida where I read one of his poems to him on one of his birthdays. I heard the rhythm of my project neighbors with English first names and Spanish last.

I speak very, very, fluent Spanish ah…

You knew who split up with whom. Momma got to name the baby she kept after she and daddy broke. I learned Spanish and hair versatility from my friends in the White high where we few colored folks congealed.

Todo 'stá bien chévere, you understand that? chévere, chévere

Black girls had our crown mastery yet my appreciation for Latinas grew when I met Wanda who everyday flipped out and switched up her follicles each seemingly indigenous. My aunt was a hairdresser and one time she got my coils so slick

His sister's Black but she is sho 'nuff pretty [but?]

that two cute Black guys passed me and said "Yeah, she's Puerto Rican" as a reason to not to talk to me, their silly segregations. My aunt was that good at hair. When I bragged to my mom she had this strange look then I felt strange. Since I was Black,

Scout who used no chart/Helped lead Lewis and Clark

Black, did that mean "mixed"? "Less Black" than us, my rural southern roots? Or that I favored my Afro-Indio grandma's grand baby, her born hair sheets of rain? Three years later no more pressings, a few years after that I stopped combing, calming, coiled kundalini haven't since.

Boogie On, Reggae Woman. What's wrong with you? Boogie on, Reggae Woman?
What you tryna do?

We put our bags and shoulders down in San Juan, took off our shoes. We salt-snacked. Then chose beds and saw where the coffee was, small pan to heat up milk, aerated the apartment with open colorful shutters. We listened to the residential part

Don't you worry 'bout a thing/Don't you worry 'bout a thing, mama

of town and changed to bedclothes. A consistent variation on a chirp or some other resonance was ubiquitous, like the earth in joyful zen. What is that sound? We played a game. What's on your playlist? I brought my laptop, it had the most on it.

So show me to where there's music/Show me to where there's music

Do you have polka? One said, trying as non-Slavics to think of music far afield. I clicked on the classic: *Who Stole the Kishka?* Not a Caribbean merengue yet a meringue, happy, rhythmic confection. They paused, what Black woman had polka on

A happy happy song

her playlist? I'm in the back seat, riding with an old friend and his family in Okinawa. The radio was on as we took a long trip. We'd gone to the house and had tea, caught up a bit and were seeing some of the non-military city. The traffic was urban American.

Kimi sasoi yobikakenu/Ai no sono

About a million songs came on the radio as we inched. The music was standard pop. One after one as caramel corn zipped from the antennae speakers of the modest old-school sedan. After a refrain the pattern was usually transparent. I'd sing along.

do-do, do-do, do-do-do, do-do-do

"How do you know all these songs?" He said after an hour or so, amazed. I thought: "They're like poems, in form" but I didn't say anything, allowing for some mystique. I thought about that moment in Old San Juan. When the polka song went off, they said:

I'm not one to make believe, I know that leaves are green

"Listen Tracie." I did. They said: What song do you have for the *coquis*? A holy PR voice. Through my mental soundscape, not even looking at my recordings. I hear these fairy frogs, messengers, welcoming us. The first we'd heard them as living. I played

I wish that I could come back as a flower

the whistled, ambient intro to "The First Garden" in Wonder's open opus, *Journey Through the Secret Life of Plants* double album. Rendered Eden. Coquis in the idyllic.

can't you see that, life's connected

Stevie's electronic acumen, sweeping world-sense—I can't prove those sounds were living coquis, but sound was a hair's breadth in that room, on the isla, that time. We heard live coquis chime with him. Sounds true. Who could say? We'd just been introduced.

send one your love...

As in Okinawa, my temporary roommates gasped and said: "How do you have something for *them*?" There's pattering for everything. I said: Always Stevie Wonder. He has a way to help us hear things. If he chose to

I am singing, of tomorrow...

recluse for the rest of his life (he *just* turned the 70 corner), this adage would be ever factual. Constant as Newton's Law. Stevie, our ears to atoms, our universe's making sound, our cosmos journeyman by secret sonics.

Is this the vision of my mind?

This Serling zone, the Rat of beginnings ushering in shock of the new, we are forced to reconcile with the losses, before 2020's lunar and solar cycle of piercing vision of confusion, seen and unseen flash the way forward.

A seed's a star's a seed

After we got through the at-random loops and sang to Chaka's hotter than hell "What I got will knock your pride aside..." even my mom said, "Wow that's a sexy song!" A woman letting her lover know she got the stuff to put a hurtin' on, she's the one

you haven't done nu-thin'

with the power, we realize Stevie wrote that. In hindsight it does sound like his but Chaka made it a sista anthem. Like many in the blue black rhythm tradition, with an emphasis on the sexier aspects of the downbeat, the wahwah

say <u>yeah</u>!

singer, the declarer, radically affects "getting in it" even with aabb lyric. Patterns guide us as can a feminist departure. The 70s songs were political and *in the pocket*. Still resonating something to us. In the moment, seeming

I know just what I say

nostalgia unlocks all the heartbreak that went into a sound, all the hope for freedom. Performance utters the speaking truth, hope for flipping the tables, yearning equality for *err-body* including this world, those we shepherd,

Jesus loves you, Children of America

failures of those who lie, to be a steady light unto the world. Post-WW2 kids, 70s sounds are a mirror held up to unnatural contradictions. The anti-umbra, neither what shines or what shows, in contrast, the brilliance. Singing along to our favorites

I can't go on this way

of the time, we hold in our stuttered weeping, elements of despair those dulcet strains sang. A few times, after I got home, alone with those earworms, I went back to how small I felt, how blanketing barometric of those social times impinged

'til I reach the higher ground

on tiny shoulders, hyperventilating for that kid afraid to leave the house with so many little bads outside, even in my own building. That time our home was robbed and it felt empty for a time after, all of the slights, horrifying situations, my own expressed

Living's just enough, just enough

cruelty. How I l honed words beyond Mother Goose pablum, my own small blades. The food insecurity of panoptical unemployment and the impoverished stores with no fresh nourishment, playing middle-class with dilapidated tv dinners.

sores cover their hands...

To open wellsprings, during this imploding year, allows me to weep for the lost, speculate on who got us to new wailing. A few, many. The activist artists playing our fears, locating our actions,

When we say you're living wrong

Our grieving, giving us hertz to keep on keeping, see things anew after the circumstances. Our sad flittering plastic gilt at having not *made* it as those few escapees, tokenized at the time seemed to, like the great Nat King, distraught eating him from inside.

I'll be standing in the wings when you check it out

What occupies me these days I never imagined even with a child wandering mind sparked by Tolkien, Le Guin's Lathe of Heaven and WBLS: Writing for a living, going to school, as a student and teacher, for a living. This is a reflecting pool year

Now some folks say that we should be—glad for what we have

why we fear, how we made it through the old tough times before. There are a few ways in which to make it through, questions beyond that basic need, how to bloom. Always lingo, vibing from a little one. Always him. All ways, Stevie.

Omnipresence

co–written with Charles Bernstein

A tree is mediated through a window, its leaves flutter up, showing their wan undersides
While all I got is this T-shirt, a spool of Jello, a free ticket to anywhere mind travels.
It is always something akin: this thread, this vein, this leaf, this plane. A through-line sewing
contrast
In the middle of a play that's been postponed, as the oatmeal rides its high horse to get out.

Or just to stay insides, barnacled by branches, cessation dropping like a leaky faucet's faucet
Symbiotic, verdancy and we, yet vernal buds' opening aspect precedes our blastocysts by eons
If an eon is a measure, what's the ego measure? One letter separates these, 7 to 14. A prime,
its double. Both gone
In a fly's ointment, tuned in turn by time's heartless amends, a peacock's cry to stationary
landing, rough sway.

This tree peels away, its song under lightning, under a cloud's darkening, yes between drops
As pent air billows unbridled in its shaft, a legion of dead leaves layering the path.
The dead leaves. Does it? Under our skin, each layer, us on the surface. Embers our kindling,
our kind, kindness.
Until the slight falters, fight alters, one time too many and all the care in the world so many
yesterdays

After spray and deluge, cloud striations mirror setting Sol, the mist sky's atmospheric
window of space-time's deep
Orations, pitched opacities in luminescent scrolls, incipient inscriptions lacerating false
detours, detonating
A flash-bang we lob to end another like ourselves, distorting the lightsound of celestial orbs,
the first word, utterling
Splits topiary tunes, fed by intransigent stares in a fantasy of unwept impossibles, hurt flares.
Then in a gush, who

Whoosh! A human flight, that sound, or someone else, or something else, aftermath utterance, cosmic exhalation.

As on a strain, but not yet to stung, of yips and yikes and yaps, lordly fights, fragrant huffs, lifting twice their weight with silvered tongues

Versed, unrehearsed, and dulcet. Set to sit in. Snare rim, Baby L's flatted foot, steel-heeled, Ohm's pulse.

Juniper buried, like simile echoes lost boast, or maybe never happened, or nobody told me, well held in song's exuberant crust.

A thrush clearing, speckled underbelly seem like seeds, a mirror of starling wings, dispersals of the world, like phonemes.

Startling things who grow to rings, rudely dissing memes, singing screams in beat to oceanic swings, sayin'—bye queens bye kings.

By gones, we like the birds, side long glances: glacé, blasé. Two monarchal boroughs, but we don't mean it. Name a nick, a shiv. We use these assignations against the grain, hyper-individual cutting words. Each of the Queens sashay, every Kings plays butoh butch

You say? I say name it, then put it in a jar and frame it (quaint never resolved no taint): brush fires rile the undermesh of desire, burning with a choir of shan't and plaints.

Plant if, a simple strain, plaintiff, assumed guilt. A wan underside of stripped flesh, lash by a tree

Shuddering, shattered, waylaid by dreams, the cost of a shift and what hold its place:

How heavy it all gets suddenly. Wait of the world to resolve these old violations; such ancient waves drown our books

In streams that riseth, stems that fail, as all at once and once in all I gather plainly, rust to a saw, crown to dog.

A corona, a ring, planet garnet, garland of spikes, uttering one time's cleave, a cur circles 'round, raised forelegs, and speaks:

I am a wig in a whirligig, fastened to the head of the meter, sunken emissary of echo and lark, sponge and spark, broken apart to come together (to gather, to tether).

Ether is most truthful hiding not even light, cumulous entity shaping in aggregate, blocking . . . is it a refracted color? Distilled empty our iris insists is a place to land?

Having fallen too far, or flung like a bent needle in Plexiglas display, lurching away from Mr.
   Protean's eclectic, voice-swathed, hypnomancy

As we decide a sliver of membrane shields us from the truth: we are mostly empty on a
   balloon, ankle-tethered, sideways-holding, thread-barest: an idea
Best left to swoon in its own gaseous bath, slivers shucked of light or, ah shucks!, I just
   worked there for an eternity and now it's my turn to dance.
Ouroboros is space wind, in that is a noun sound, it reverbs and all the colors blind in the
   fullness of the shaking, spectrum beyond the orb's totalizing pupil—
Every time you say so—shuns liberty for liberty's lore, the old tune gone rancid, getting jump
   on next week's junk

Scent in this vacuum, subatomic, slings back olfacts through memory, bullying the brain a
   piece of humankind, limits to the work of skin, viscera, interpretation:
Gun-shy then gunned down, lickety splat. The mouse, the clock, and me (um, er, us), frozen
   in time's fissures, pointing at blank, losing it.
Where does the one eye direct itself when thinking? Why there? Why does it loll, when
   "checking out"?
I wish I knew, sung to "The Martians Are Landing in Palm Beach but I'm in Palm Springs."

All the sand grains are < than galactic pinpricks and yet we bleed trying to reach out, rather
   than clutching
At falls, gangrene, and lace, aboard the incandescent train, hurtling between gravity and
   politesse, hiccups and fresh spring water.
What falls between what we readily grasp? The dog's nose is 10,000x more sensitive than "the
   master"
Yet not as fast as the unknown, which, in slick of a sec, interweaves its Heavenward alarm,
   amelioration and chagrin, hand in hand.

We walk curs quickly and then rush back in. Everly pulling them away from their whole
   world, yet they perpetually love
Beats the everly indifferent 13 out of 7 times, as the saying might go, during this longingly
   sullen fright of the soul.

Lucky numbers give balm to the spirit. What's spritely? Sport in the soul? What makes the heart leap
To soiled profusion, animating burrows? Ill-timed, timid blame: procrustean swerves amidst anaphylactic reverses.

When one knocks, there's that catch. A latch to each door of a beat, a valve to ventricle: filling discrete parts, building up
Only to tear down the stairs crying "help's on the way," but thinking, What way? Whose way? From where? How's that?
A house feels a tap. Is this where the heart lives? Coursing: drains, fills, heats then plumbs. A hum syncs all *mmms* under.
"Lines on liver" like trap that forgave itself, both of us, not everyone as let's keep it close: a plump dinger if ever I did saw one.

Glean of chrome is the tuner to the marble, sparkling abrasive cleanser. A paste made of dust, clay, liquid life. All is safe to consume—
But gives me no pause anyway, how, or where; just don't try it at home. Fled to the ledge but the whatchamacallit was ahead, anyway tracks of its traces.
Is that a speck of something? Of green? Against a gray cloud its verdancy strikes me
Like a motor who needs its wheel, a voter its votes, the penguin the snow.

This is veracity. True hues exist only with another. Blindness is a reduced broth, pan of simple shades.
Munched on Aeolian aerogrammes, full frontal driftlessness, sings this one praise till it becomes sweetest thread of smelling salt.
Our Lot in life, our Himalayan death: K2, popinJay sicc's sick sycophants, uphill. I foresaw, H8
As or when or if the orchestra becomes single sound, singed in the fire of unkeeping

Other letters, feathering a tower, a monument's marbleized confection of snaking lies, startlings.
Can or concoct, edging out, tight play to incapacity's derelict delights, hanging by a tread.

A Cagean footfell, bliss night before plowing, lower regions, aerating sky, flickers. Its finger a
pointed mark. A grooved fate line, faulting.
Hear, O, Whaddyacallit? The law shatters on lawns of intransigence, severs the bodies politic:
fair never indifference, *truth* in balance.

A Solomonic bone held upside like a baby's toe, like fallen Odin. In my mind the hanged
man is always darker, closer to the tree's color, from which he's looped, like Jesus's hair.
The contrast of white tresses, like the fey, a griffin's wray of light to show shadows.
Pockmarked for the trial of the trail, mental fight, garden of earthen gradations—
Notions of shape and fear. In this reversal, the least hued dangle by the petard. Dogmatic, by
Fenrir's demise.

Abstraction fails me, faint trance hard by overblown estuary, listless lyric trace.
Eternity's sills crack with cries: as if to mourn, to weep, to shake fists, to ignite fires, to hold
accountable, to per-sever-e.
Each crystalline petal is lucent until the edge. Its hardness crunches like a hyperventilated
nostril's rim.
Eye's habit of time, going back and the rebuff, doubletakes on the bluff, hanging promontory
of infinite proclivities

On which to dance, to sing, to shout, to cry, to jump, to exclaim, to shake, to bounce, to scream,
to leap, to twirl, to spin, to run!
What is one willing to do to sense anything? What's one willing to consume in the frail
sense of self, ouroboros?
I came to you out of the storm, you said, and then I could not find you.
Or wouldn't, surging through self-forming conduits, spirals made of gaseous eruptions,
aspirations expiring like so many sitting muckamucks

All these lightning looks, shaking the ground, connecting others: Sowelu, that potter's child,
Shango.
What is the shattering of bright about? The imprint on mind, Lichtenberg's draw. They say
They disappear after a little while, a day. I wonder: Do they? submerge. What does the heart
beat after

Being rattled? Does love shake out? Do corazón tendrils everywhere inspissate? Do the two
    brain halves become

More sentient? Do gut bacteria, with draping veins over stomach, couple, double, arising
    hunger?
Plasma is psalms in the electric box. A poem sears beyond Sol's capacity. We sound out Oh my
    god. My God.
The tapping of a toe is a ripple, shaped as a question. Any sound as we hold our breath for
    God's eardrum
To strike. The vocal folds to open saying *aaaah*, we hope and await in Sheol. Muscles ache,
    stones may crack—

But it's we that forsake, turn away, forget, even forgive, for giving can be as much denial as
    vengeance. A turning that knows no place to
Stop, sputtering like mad hatters without hats. There's gold in them hills if you think about it
    long enough,
Diamonds and broccoli. Pretty soon the days before the war became much like the days that
    followed, no that can't be right, such splendid dissolution
Cornering the blinds in record time, hopping for hoops, hoping along placidly, not a heart in
    sight, but you can hear them wherever you look.

The silence inside the sound smacks of rhythm, lunatic embrace of the slope's grace, as beats
    entwined by cobbles
A broken man and a small stone. Gargantua New York roars back they say. Always the big dog
    (a little isle).
Quizzical, stuck-up, you almost veer to course; autopilot permanently disabled, senses on brink
Under word arrest in flagrant ammonia of extraterrestrial waferings

Till granite is the soft part, the near side of aroma
Sudsy hollers in multiplying rumors, hovers jubilant, gracious, unabetted
Clunky admonitions, rehearsals, blustering defiance, in defense of jest, coolly unbecoming
    ministrations
Nickeled, dimed, and quartered to an inch of a new life, leapt in space.

A star focuses a boy. *Pobrecito*, he is coughing, he's hacking, our affectionate name for seats-
for-hire rumbling.
This child aims at empire symbol, in sputum refuses to give, his discards part of the city's fauna.
Refusing, to relent there is a promise in him he stubbornly stays. Mother taught him better
than to give
away the only thing that matters, his soul to keep. He has a twin, who doesn't hold a
smoothed surface. She cups

his luminous eyes, deciding to wave her hand for harbor, will welcome love in. They switch
places.
A cosmic tango, or is it imbroglio?, incorrigible summit, [poke in the eye of change] *times*
[bone-cold fluster]
Small-stoned streets are not the same as brooked sideways. Roots burrow humankind's
arrogant facade
on shifting, hard sand. Time will say they hum, even as they are axed to nubs, tendrils unify
and upend plastic piping.

Dips: sure don't feel that way. History's not born but made, hits hard either way. Alluvial as
the will of a tick with tricks enough for a lifetime.
Don't spin me round, don't spin me around
There is a substratum communion, in the mantle, below the cap crust. It's a bellow sound,
under standing.
Oh elephantine, oh whaling. What loss we have as we trim the range of your continental ears.

Terror in calm, in claim, in compulsory subordination as suborning abjection, in the
stuttering, licentious larceny of imagination's acts
In the all-night vigil of quested care, wrested impudence, and driftward mobilization.
Full-well invested with *not right* but just, *not good* but delight, *not authority* but that which
permeates it.
In the ludicrous leap from here to here, neither way nor means, copping to a plea.

Cages imprison waves in sheetrock, asbestos bubbles implode the references of the known
breath of this sphere.

Illumined without visible light, teetering in woven pleats, guided by the heart's gondolas.
In typical sapient fashion they diligent new terras to poison in wisdom's name. The actual
    omnipresent wise say: *uhhhn.*
Silk shuffle of insolvent handiwork, gold standard of syncretic necessity.

There is corollary relief sense at winning the microbial war. Naked apes already lose, filled
    with whom they seek, themselves.
Parasitic on two legs, how don't they fall? Molten center floods its commentary awaiting the
    new round of species overtakers.
Non compos mentis tucked inside *however possible*, runner-up to the runner-up in asymptotic
    glory:
Surely, truly, absolutely, positively, certainly, you bet, you got it, BINGO!, bull's-eye!, homer!

Lightning charges deep elements. Fire, Pleistocene water, remains of hydrofourocarbon resin,
    unstable nuclei—
Oneiric license for tintinnabulation. Did you boil the water?
A ball shifts its scalp around Sol. The blinding god is disinterested until it embraces. As earth
    will take us in, so does
the outstretching, consuming eye.

It flickers and licks us clean. Its cupping, unlike our her here, is convexed. Some kind of swat.
    Some kind of play.
You know: *olly olly out and free; switch maps, break prosody's back; I wander cozy as a shroud.*
I wonder where jacks came from? That metaphysical game. At what age do we tire? At what
    point do we fear
the metaphor? An engulfing *mano*, the delay. A second of frivolity we take seriously at one
    point.

Gelling intention and particularized dexterity, how marginal our opposable digit ends up being.
And all the time just *seaming*, one perception jostling close by whippersnappers.
We are flecks in a galactic sequence and so we make something of it. We ripple earth,
    droplets, zephyrs, as rapidly as a cinch.

acknowledgements

401 Requiem was published in *The Paris Review*, Issue 236, Spring 2021.

A slightly different version of **2016 Requiescat Break** was published in *The Iowa Review*, Vol. 51, Issue 2, 2022.

Acclimate was published in the *ANDYSWIPE Anthology*, Rogue Scholars Press, Jan. 2021.

Arwald the King and an earlier version of **There's Always Time** were published in *Paideuma*, Vol. 47, Symposium: Literature and War, edited by Benjamin Friedlander, 2022.

Canon Cannon Memoria is an erasure piece prompted by Steve Cannon's prose poem "Untitled ("Meditation on Miles")," published in *The Iowa Review*, Vol. 51, Issue 2, Spring 2022.

Feeling Brought In: Sketching Flexing, Fluxus, Flexibility and Afro-futurist Seeing of Dick Higgins was published in *The Improbable*, Vol. 1, No. 1: Time Indefinite, published by Siglio Press, October, 2020.

Griner Grounding and **There's Always Time** were published by *Brooklyn Rail*, July-August, 2022.

Kenning-Beginning was published in *Word: An Anthology by A Gathering of the Tribes*, Gathering of the Tribes Inc., 2017.

An earlier version of **Night time is the _____ time** was published in *Exacting Clam*, No. 6, Autumn 2022.

The form of **The Occasions: Zhuitsu Wonder** was prompted by a conversation with poet Khadijah Queen in 2020.

Omnipresence was originally published in *Conjunctions*, Vol. 77, States of Play: The Games Issue, Fall 2021.

An orated version of **Prism** was presented in my short film, *Black Spring*, that premiered in 2021, commissioned by the Obermann Center and the Department of Cinematic Arts, University of Iowa.

An earlier version of **Snapshot: Bikini Et Al** was published in the anthology *Oh Sandy! A Remembrance*, Rail Editions, 2015.

Steel Away is the page-based version of "New Steel," a song I wrote and performed for the morrisharp recording *Duality*, ZoAr Records, 2021.

Sum. / 'Too Oh (under another title) and **To Poem Inside Darkly** were published in *Black Poetry Review*, Issue 1, Summer 2020.

Tragedies in Acts: Avoiding Emmett Till at Furious Flower's Blacksonian is in conversation with a poem that I'm now having difficulty tracking down, by the artist Jo Stewart. "Tragedies in Acts" was published in *Interim*, Vol. 37, Issue 3-4, On Black Aliveness, edited by Ronaldo V. Wilson, 2020.

The untitled *linked senryu* series was published in *The Iowa Review*, Vol. 50, Issue 3, Winter 2020/21.